"It has been my great pleasure to work with Rick Fisher. God has used him powerfully as a pastor and as an encourager of leaders. But most importantly, Rick and Debbie Fisher have understood that if your family chooses not to follow your God, then a shadow falls on every other accomplishment you might have enjoyed. This book is filled with godly, wise, inspirational counsel about one of life's most important undertakings: legacy. I wholeheartedly recommend it!"

– Dr. Henry Blackaby, author of *Experiencing God.*

"The world calls us to celebrate awards, promotions, wealth, and recognition—all things that are fleeting. Seldom do we hear the call of this book: to leave a legacy by growing a godly family. Through biblical teachings and personal examples, Rick Fisher (and his wife, Debbie) allow us to walk with them and learn from their experiences as Christian parents. I encourage all parents—and parents to-be—to read this book."

– Dr. Chuck Lawless, Dean of Doctoral Studies, Vice-President for Spiritual Formation and Ministry Centers, Southeastern Baptist Theological Seminary

"I've known Rick and Debbie Fisher for more than 20 years. We have been together many times and often around the ministry of prayer. As you read their book, you too will have the pleasure of being with them in a ministry of prayer. Their lives exemplify a deep love-life for their Lord. They model a life, a marriage, and a family that has a personal relationship with a living God. I'm grateful for their transparency, for their sharing about their personal journey of prayer and for their encouragement and challenge to seek to join God in a covenant for the next generations."

– Rev. Johnny Rumbough, Executive Director of Missions, Lexington, South Carolina

"In this book, Rick Fisher reminds us that we are both receivers and givers of the great family inheritance of faith. He challenges us to teach our children by example the importance of knowing and sharing the love, power, and forgiveness of the Lord. From generation to generation, the most important inheritance we can receive or give is living in this incomparable blessing our family has passed down. You're going to cherish the sweet and powerful message of this book from Rick's heart!"

– Dr. Evans P. Whitaker, President, Anderson University

FROM GENERATION TO GENERATION

BUILDING A GODLY LEGACY

"ONE GENERATION SHALL PRAISE YOUR WORKS TO
ANOTHER AND SHALL DECLARE YOUR MIGHTY ACTS."
PSALM 145:4

Rick Fisher

Blackaby Ministries International
Jonesboro, Georgia

FROM GENERATION TO GENERATION: BUILDING A GODLY LEGACY
PUBLISHED BY BLACKABY MINISTRIES INTERNATIONAL
P.O. Box 1035
Jonesboro, GA 30237
www.blackaby.org

ISBN: 978-1-7338536-9-9

Publisher's Cataloging-in-Publication Data

Names: Fisher, Rick, author.
Title: From generation to generation : building a Godly legacy / Rick Fisher.
Description: Includes bibliographical references. | Jonesboro, GA: Blackaby Ministries International, 2020.
Identifiers: LCCN 2020909613 | ISBN 978-1-7338536-9-9
Subjects: LCSH Christian life. | Families--Biblical teaching. | Child rearing--Religious aspects--Christianity. | Families--Religious life. | BISAC RELIGION / Christian Living / Family & Relationships | RELIGION / Christian Living / Prayer | RELIGION / Christian Life / Relationships
Classification: LCC BV4526.2 .F57 2020 | DDC 248.4--dc23

Printed in the United States of America
2020 — 1st ed

Contents

Dedication

To my grandparents Ernest and Altha for praying over my life.

To my parents, Tommy and Betty, for living out their faith in front of me.

To my wife, Debbie, for walking beside me in this great adventure of life.

To my girls, Jamie and Betsy, for loving their dad and tolerating his OCD!

To my sons-in-law, Rob and Lucas, for loving my girls and leading their families to follow Jesus.

To my grandchildren, Thomas, Ashley, Jase, Leighton, and Gray, for being the delightful people whose lives encourage me about the next generations of our family.

I love each of you!

FOREWORD

Over the years, many people have asked me what it was like growing up in the home of a spiritual giant like my father, Henry Blackaby. Depending on how much time we have, I answer that question in a variety of ways. The first thing I generally mention is that my dad could never have become the spiritual colossus he did if he had not enjoyed my mother's wholehearted support and encouragement. The second thing I say is that neither my father nor my mother was a perfect parent. In fact, they were far from it at times! Nevertheless, God has the capacity to take ordinary, flawed parents and create homes that cultivate spiritual vibrancy, perseverance, and joy.

A third thing I usually state is that all four of my siblings and I attended seminary and serve the Lord. At last count, we have collected nine seminary degrees and seven college degrees. No mean feat, considering my parents earned a paltry mission pastor's wage, and the thought of starting a college fund would have appeared ludicrous to them. Yet, though all five children serve the Lord to this day, we have each done so in a unique way with diverse skills and interests. While it is one thing to say that my parents walked closely with the Lord, it is another to state that all five of their children have followed in their footsteps.

If there is time for a lengthier discussion, I will also note that my dad did not develop his faith in a vacuum. If you ask him who the greatest spiritual influence in his life was, he will quickly mention his father, G.R.S. Blackaby. His father was a bank manager and a lay preacher. He was a man of strong convictions. He fought in many of the major battles of World War One. He rigorously practiced his faith even amid the horrors of losing friends in trench warfare. After the war, when G.R.S. Blackaby could not find a church that met his standards, he started one himself. At one point, my grandfather rented a dance hall to hold church services. My grandmother played the piano. The three children formed the congregation. My father still remembers sitting in that hall and listening to his father passionately urge his family to live their lives wholeheartedly for Christ.

But my grandfather's faith was not self-made either, though it was certainly well maintained. My great-grandfather Blackaby was a Christian businessman. He owned his own bakery and was a pillar of his local Baptist church in England. As a young man, he and his two brothers went to college. But not just any college. They attended Spurgeon's College while Charles Spurgeon led it. My great-grandfather's two brothers became pastors, while he became a godly layman.

As far up the Blackaby family tree as you go, you will find a legacy of godliness. Not all of my ancestors were devout Christians. One was a revolutionary during the Chartist Rebellion. Another was sent to Australia for seven years for thievery. But the vast majority of my direct family members were devout Christians who passed on their faith to the next generation.

It has been said that society is always just one generation away from complete paganism. It only takes one generation of Christians failing to pass on their faith for an entire population to degenerate into rebellion against its Creator. Parents must diligently teach their children to walk with God. My parents didn't just take me to church each week. They demonstrated what an experience with God looks like. We talked about God around the dinner table. As we drove places in our vehicle, we discussed God's activity in our lives. I heard my parents talk to God in prayer. I saw the glow on their faces as they served the Lord and experienced His joy. My father often said that he committed himself to walk so closely and vibrantly with his Lord that when his children watched his life, they would desire to have a similar relationship with God themselves. He succeeded.

Many things about my Christian life came easily for me, not because I was particularly godly but because they were generously handed down to me from my ancestors. Hearing God speak became routine, because my relatives had all heard from Him. Obeying God was assumed, because I never witnessed my parents *disobey* Him. Spending time with God was valued, because whenever I rose early in the morning I found that my father had risen even earlier to spend time with his Savior.

Make no mistake. Rearing godly offspring may well be the most difficult thing you ever attempt. God was a father figure to Adam and Eve, yet they rebelled against Him. Adam's son murdered his brother. Isaac's son deceived him and cheated his brother. Jacob's sons lied to him and sold their brother into slavery. The high priest Eli's sons were so evil God sentenced them to death. Samuel's sons were a disaster. David's son Absalom murdered his brother Amnon and launched a civil war against his father. Joram had the good king Jehoshaphat for a father, but he chose to follow after his father-in-law, King Ahab, instead. King Hezekiah was one of Judah's godliest kings, but he raised Manasseh, one of Judah's wickedest monarchs. King Josiah was godly, but his children were so evil that God determined to judge the land during their rule. What does this historical overview suggest? Even when you are a devout follower of God, it is not easy to rear your children to follow Christ as closely as you do.

I have always been inspired by what King David did for his son Solomon. Solomon, when he was older, strayed from the Lord, but he got off to an amazing start. How? Much of the answer comes from his father, David:

> So David gave orders to gather the resident aliens that were in the land of Israel, and he appointed stonecutters to cut finished stones for building God's house. David supplied a great deal of iron to make the nails for the doors of the gates and for the fittings, together with an immeasurable quantity of bronze, and innumerable cedar logs because the Sidonians and Tyrians had brought a large quantity

of cedar logs to David. David said, "My son Solomon is young and inexperienced, and the house that is to be built for the Lord must be exceedingly great and famous and glorious in all the lands. Therefore, I will make provision for it." So David made lavish preparations for it before his death. (1 **Chron.** 22:2-5)

David knew that he would die before his son Solomon experienced all God intended for him. David could not prolong his life, but he could extend his influence. So, he gathered all manner of resources for Solomon. David also gave Solomon godly advice (1 **Kings** 2:1-9). David advised his son, *"Above all, may the Lord give you insight and understanding when He puts you in charge of Israel. . ."* (1 **Chron.** 22:12). Then, shortly before he died, David told Solomon, *". . . for you are a wise man . . ."* (1 **Kings** 2:9). It is not surprising, then, that when God offered to grant Solomon whatever he asked, the young king requested wisdom (1 **Kings** 3:9). After all, his father had assured him he was wise enough to pursue it.

I believe that a large part of our spiritual legacy involves the spiritual resources we leave our children. God intended for Solomon to build a magnificent temple, so his father, David, left behind extensive building supplies perfectly suited for that purpose. The problem for many families is that the parents concern themselves with leaving savings accounts and property for their children, not spiritual treasure. Their heirs might be financially wealthy, but they are spiritual paupers.

I am so pleased that my friend and associate Rick Fisher wrote *From Generation to Generation: Building a Godly Legacy*. I am excited about this book for several reasons. First, it addresses an enormous need. A recent study revealed that two-thirds of people who regularly attend church as high school students will leave the faith before they graduate from college. A 66% casualty rate of the Church's young people is appalling! Fisher wrote this book at a crucial time when Christians are desperately wanting to "get it right" with their families.

Second, I have known Rick and Debbie Fisher for many years. Rick is the Vice President of Blackaby Ministries International, the organization of which I am president. He and I travel around the world speaking at conferences together. We have shared many heartfelt conversations. Rick is a student of God's Word and knows it well. He has poured over the Bible's teaching on families. He served as a pastor for thirty years and ministered to countless families as they navigated the complexities of parenthood. But, most importantly, Rick and Debbie have two amazing daughters who love and serve the Lord and are now parenting their own children to do the same. What Rick teaches in this book does not stem from a theory but from his own successful experience.

Third, parents constantly ask me for suggestions or advice on how to rear godly children. Now I have a book I can place in people's hands! Of all the subjects you might read about, few have more significant consequences than this one. Don't be like those Christian parents who knows the batting averages of their favorite team but cannot point to any verses on how to rear their children! This book matters.

I hope you will read this book carefully and prayerfully. It was written out of love and concern. It was composed by people who know what they are talking about and who back up their claims with a successful track record. Most importantly, this book is based on the timeless truths of Scripture that never go out of date or need updating.

I pray God will bless you and your family as you read the following pages. Be assured that God loves your family even more than you do, and He will do everything necessary to reveal truths to you that will richly bless your home. Trust Him with your family. Listen to what He says. Do what He tells you. And be blessed.

Dr. Richard Blackaby
President, Blackaby Ministries International
Co-Author, *Experiencing God*, *Rebellious Parenting*, *Experiencing God at Home*

CHAPTER 1

Introduction

I grew up in a family that had a deep faith in God and demonstrated that faith in their homes, churches, and workplaces. Living in that godly atmosphere shaped me in many ways. It instilled in me an understanding of sin and my need to surrender my life to Christ. During a revival service at my home church when I was eight years old, God prompted me to address my sin. I prayed with my grandmother at the altar, and my spiritual destiny changed forever.

My journey of faith has continued throughout the subsequent 55+ years. It has been marked by powerful moments when I encountered God's truth and deepened my relationship with Him. But there have been challenging times as well when I allowed apathy, confusion, and neglect to seep into my relationship with Christ. On those occasions, God used the legacy of my godly family members to remind me there is no higher purpose in life than walking daily with Him.

During my early years as a father, God helped me recognize the futility of relying on my own best thinking or efforts as a parent. I tried to dedicate my daughters to the Lord each day, but several years passed before I realized my deeper responsibility to live out my faith in practical ways before my children. With God's help and by His grace, I believe I got it right more often than I got it wrong. As I write these words, the girls are 37 and 41 with families of their own. They have married godly men and are rearing their five children to live out the faith my wife, Debbie, and I passed to them.

When I became a grandfather, one of my first thoughts was that I wished I had understood the importance of passing on a godly legacy when my daughters were born. But God has used lessons from the past to prepare my wife and me for today. I pray these words encourage you and challenge you to invest your life in the next generations God has given you the opportunity and stewardship to influence.

CHAPTER 2

Down On Their Knees

My grandfather was a "tent revivalist," an itinerant evangelist who traveled through the towns and villages of western North Carolina. He would spread sawdust on the ground, pitch a tent, and teach singing schools during the day for anyone who wanted to attend. He preached the gospel each night, challenging the congregation to surrender their lives to Jesus. My mother and her seven siblings were the choir. To this day, the hymn my grandfather sang at the end of every service, "What a Friend We Have in Jesus," stirs something in my soul.

During my early childhood, when my parents both worked full-time jobs, I spent a lot of time with both sets of grandparents (we all lived in the North Carolina mountain town of Sylva). One of my most vivid memories from those years is of a night I spent in the cinder-block house where my tent-preaching grandfather and grandmother lived. The walls were paper thin, so I could hear most of what happened in the house during the night. Having drifted off to sleep, I woke up to the sound of my grandparents' voices across the hall. I soon realized they were not talking to each other but to God. I later learned they were on their knees, a posture they assumed every night, crying out to God for their lives, ministry, and family.

At one point during their prayer, they called out each of their grandchildren's names, and my ears tuned in more closely. When they called my name and asked God to work in my life, my heart beat faster, but I did not really understand what was happening spiritually. I struggled to fall asleep after that episode, and years passed before I truly appreciated what happened that night. My grandparents were living out the truth of **Ezekiel 22:30.** They were "standing in the gap" on behalf of their family. They were building a wall of prayer, creating a spiritual legacy that influences our family to this day.

CHAPTER 3

Making an Investment

Legacy is an important word to me. It is easy to be caught up in our culture's obsession with building and leaving an inheritance of money and material goods. In the busyness of life, Christ's followers must understand that, while an inheritance consists of things (houses, land, money, possessions) we leave for loved ones, a legacy is what we instill in them. It is unlikely that many people living today can remember my grandfather's sermons or my grandmother's testimonies, but enumerable people have been affected by their five grandsons who have served as pastors and the family members who have ministered as leaders in their churches, workplaces, and communities.

When my time on earth ends, my degrees, positions of service, and recognitions will be meaningless. My legacy will be evident not by my personal accomplishments but by my investment in others. Was I an effective steward of the people God placed in my life, those He called me to influence for Him and His glory? Did I take advantage of God-given opportunities to pour into my family, or was I distracted by my pursuit of positions and possessions?

Contemporary culture offers little encouragement to those who prioritize building a spiritual legacy over personal comfort and self-gain. Few will stand and applaud parents and grandparents who choose to live according to eternal truths and principles that are contrary to popular opinion and practice. The drumbeat to which society marches emanates from the prince of this world, and he desires to damage and destroy all that is good and godly.

Recent studies indicate that more than 65% of children who grow up attending church will walk away from their faith before they graduate from college. When a few years of higher education can dismantle 18 years of church attendance, as Barney Fife would so eloquently say, "we have a situation on our hands." Of course, some of the wanderers later return. But my experience has shown that many of those who return are drawn to the institution of the Church rather than to Christ. In more than 30 years of ministry in the local church, I have heard many parents express a heartfelt desire to rear their children in the Church. However, I have watched many of those parents drop their children off at the church for Bible studies and fun activities and return an hour or two later to take them home, seemingly oblivious to the "do what I say, not what I do" contradiction in their behavior. There seems to be a disconnect between religion and relationship. Many busters and millennials view the Church as something that will help their kids turn out right but have little or no interest in the Church themselves or its relevancy to daily life. But be aware. The old adage is true: the apple does not fall far from the tree.

CHAPTER 4

Who Wants Them?

S everal years ago, I spoke in North Carolina for my friend David Spray. The church had a strategically placed banner in the hallway outside the worship center. The words on the banner caught my attention and set in motion a determined pursuit of what the banner implied. These were the convicting words written on it: "Whoever wants the next generation the most will get them." Simple, yet powerful!

I have never been particularly impressed by trite clichés that sound good but prompt no significant action. Yet God used the words on that banner to judge my attitudes, priorities, words, and behavior. Is my desire for my family to follow Jesus greater than the evil forces that desire to destroy them? Am I willing to surrender my will to God, allowing Him to work in my life so my children and grandchildren can watch me follow Jesus and desire to follow Him too? Do I respond to life's challenges with faith and confidence in the God who loves them more than I ever could? Do I really want to do whatever it takes to claim the next generations of my family for Jesus?

Several years ago, God brought to my mind (through Dr. Henry Blackaby's teachings) a Scripture passage I had read many times but not fully understood or embraced: **Isaiah 59:21**. In that verse, God promises to enter into a covenant with those who honor Him and live according to His precepts: "'As for me,' says the Lord, 'this is My covenant with them: My Spirit who is upon you, and My words which I have put in your mouth, shall not depart from your mouth, nor from the mouth of your descendants, nor from the mouth of your descendants' descendants,' says the Lord, 'from this time and forevermore.'" What an amazing covenant He offers to His people, that as we honor Him in our lives, He will honor and preserve His name in our family from generation to generation.

As I read those words, I realized that the God of Heaven was offering me His limitless power, grace, and faithfulness if I honored Him with my life. And His resources were available and ready to be released into my family! I found myself remembering the words of Joshua as he stood in the Promised Land and declared, "Choose for yourselves this day whom you will serve ... but as for me and my house, we will serve the Lord" (**Joshua 24:15**). My desire to know and serve the Lord has increasingly become the driving force of my life. I long to see my family come to love, honor, and serve the Lord for generations to come, and the covenant-keeping God stands ready to join me (and you) in bringing this passion to fruition!

CHAPTER 5

Setting Our Priorities

The most important gift God has given us besides eternal and abundant life is our family. We must embrace the spiritual responsibility that comes with that gift, because our commitment to our family will affect the way we live, our priorities, and the decisions we make. The degree to which we live out our faith in front of our family will shape the way they understand, know, and experience God.

Establishing a spiritual legacy while living in a culture filled with relativism and self-centeredness is challenging. In fact, it is one of the most challenging roles we have as parents and grandparents. Our calling to our family is filled with difficulties we must endure, mistakes we must make right, lessons we often learn through pain, tough love, and embracing the power of forgiveness and reconciliation. It is a journey that is impossible without

God's help. If teaching and rearing God-honoring children and grandchildren is our life passion, however, this covenant-keeping God comes alongside us to do in and through us what we could never accomplish with our best thinking or in our own strength. We are on the front lines. I believe each person who desires to see the next generations walk with God must recognize at least two significant responsibilities.

(1) **We are called to insulate our families from the foolish thinking around them.** Notice I did not say "isolate" our families. As Scripture indicates, we are to live in the world, yet not be of the world. Thus, we must use our children's formative years to invest in them and prepare them to engage with their world while providing a safe haven for them within our homes.

In **Colossians 2:6-8**, Paul gives this challenge: "As you therefore have received Christ Jesus the Lord, so walk in Him, rooted and built up in Him and established in the faith, as you have been taught, abounding in it with thanksgiving. Beware lest anyone cheat you through philosophy and empty deceit, according to the tradition of men, according to the basic principles of the world, and not according to Christ." Spiritual leaders in the home—whether parents or grandparents—are called to live exemplary spiritual lives before the next generations. And we must do so in such a manner that they clearly see the reality of God's truth lived out in us. To fulfil this role, we must guard our hearts and minds through a disciplined, daily walk with Christ so we are not swayed by the deceitfulness of today's culture. Paul challenged us to walk in Christ, to be "built up in Him and established in the faith" so our lives reflect God's truth to the next generations.

Ezekiel 33 is another passage that has challenged me as a father and grandfather. While the situation spiritual leaders face today differs from the one the passage describes—we are not in a physical battle that requires a watchman—the principles of a watchman's role remain relevant.

The watchman Ezekiel 33 references must be uniquely trained to recognize the advancing enemy, knowing when and how to sound the alarm for those he is called to protect. His responsibility is a matter of life and death. God has challenged me to be a spiritual watchman for my family, always alert to what is going on around them. Not only do I need to be aware of my role to stand spiritual guard for my family but also of the tragic consequences that will befall them if I fail to give a clear warning, instruction, or example.

As a parent and grandparent, I must continue to mature spiritually. When I fail to grow, others suffer. I cannot relate to my four-year-old grandson in the same manner I relate to my eight-year-old granddaughter or 41-year-old daughter. One of the challenges of building a spiritual legacy is embracing the reality that previous victory does not guarantee future success. I must continue to improve my skills and deepen my relationship with God in order to fulfill my role as a watchman. Never diminish your important responsibility to your family. Never underestimate the significance of God speaking into your life as you pray and read His Word. Understand and embrace the tremendous impact you can have on the people God has called you to lead.

(2) **We are called to prepare our families to live with a personal trust in Jesus and a growing understanding of God's Word.** Scripture tells us that God has predisposed children to learn from their parents and grandparents. In **Deuteronomy 6:4-7**, God speaks directly to His people about their role in the family: "Hear, O Israel: The Lord our God, the Lord is one! You shall love the Lord your God with all your heart, with all your soul and with all your strength. And these words which I command you today shall be in your heart. You shall teach them diligently to your children and shall talk of them when you sit in your house, when you walk by the way, when you lie down and when you rise up." A complementary passage in **Ephesians 6:4** speaks specifically to fathers: "And you, fathers, do not provoke your children to wrath, but bring them up in the training and admonition of the Lord."

The most important aspect of the legacy we leave is intentionally seeking to raise up the next generations to follow Christ and live God-honoring lives. God gave children a longing to learn, and if we do not meet that desire, they will search for answers elsewhere. We must ask ourselves this question: will we embrace our role as spiritual teachers or will we surrender it to potentially ungodly influences? The primary source of spiritual instruction for the next generations is not the classroom, community programs, or youth ministry at the local church. It is found in the home. God commands parents and grandparents to create an atmosphere of example and instruction whereby the next generations can come to know and love Him.

We would not think of letting our children learn to walk or talk on their own. We spend many hours helping, instructing, and encouraging them in those areas. As they grow, we teach them how to throw and hit a ball, drive a car, make wise financial decisions, and much more. Why, then, would we leave them to figure out life's most important questions on their own?

I love to watch what my grandchildren do. It is wonderful if they excel at sports, learn to play an instrument, or graduate with honors. But what if they experience all those things but do not develop a personal relationship with Jesus? What if they don't love the Lord their God with all their heart, soul, mind, and strength?

If we make the commitment, pay the price, and engage the assignment, we can join the covenant-keeping God in teaching the next generations to love and serve Him. We have the amazing privilege each day to write on the pages of their lives and impact the future.

My friend Henry Blackaby lists this among his life goals: "I want to live my life in such a manner that my children and grandchildren want to follow and serve the

God they see their father and grandfather following and serving." Do you have the same desire for your family?

CHAPTER 6

Spiritual Culture Shock

I grew up in a sheltered environment. I spent most of my time with church friends doing church activities. Because my parents took seriously their calling to bring me up in the instruction of the Lord and in the community of faith, I came to know Jesus as my Savior at the age of eight and surrendered my life to vocational ministry when I was 15 years old.

In light of my call to ministry, I decided to attend Gardner-Webb College (now Gardner-Webb University) rather than following through with my original plan to attend the University of North Carolina at Chapel Hill. When I arrived on the GWC campus, I found myself outside the boundaries of my sheltered upbringing and had the opportunity to make my own choices. While this newfound freedom presented its own set of challenges (some I handled well and some I did not, though that's another book!), my time in the classroom presented an unexpected crossroads moment.

Dr. Vann Murrell, my New Testament professor, taught me many amazing lessons during my freshman year. He was a transparent Christian, and I can still remember his passionate prayers at the beginning of each class. I was a little uncomfortable at first, because I was not accustomed to listening to someone encounter God so personally. But that experience has continued to influence my understanding of what God desires for each of us in our relationship with Him, especially in the area of prayer.

Dr. Murrell was a conservative theologian, but he shared not only his own conservative interpretation of the life and teachings of Jesus and the New Testament writers but also differing views. For me, his classes led to a somewhat shocking revelation—there are many different views of Scripture and people who actually embrace them!

As I wrapped my mind and heart around this reality, I found myself questioning not only what I believed but also why I believed what I did. While my family had influenced me positively by teaching and living spiritual truth, this revelation made me keenly aware that my beliefs were based more on my family's faith than on my personal encounters with God and His Word. I needed to develop my own worldview.

As I reflect on those days, I am thankful for the faith my family passed on to me. While I could not relate to

God based solely on their walk of faith, their example paved the way for my own personal journey. If I had not had them as positive role models, I would have been more easily swayed by the ungodly interpretations of Scripture I encountered from various "fringe religious groups" during college. A verse that impacts me today as I consider the example I am setting for my family is **Ephesians 5:1-2**: "Therefore be imitators of God as dear children. And walk in love, as Christ also has loved us and given Himself for us, an offering and a sacrifice to God for a sweet-smelling aroma." Our past influences us, but we live in the present. God placed us here for some specific purposes, and we can be certain that one of them is to build and leave behind a godly legacy. Let me add, God's purpose for your life may be to restore a spiritual legacy previous generations have damaged or broken. God may also intend for you to be the first person in your family to establish a godly legacy that will influence others for decades.

One of the most powerful times in my ministry was when I became the senior pastor of Lexington Baptist Church in Lexington, South Carolina. As our community grew, Lexington became a popular destination for families looking for good schools, great neighborhoods, and convenient shopping. Through this growth, God showed me that people spend lots of energy and resources trying to be comfortable, and we often equate order and stability in the visible things of life with inner peace. But God's Kingdom does not work that way. His agenda has always been countercultural. Jesus said, "If anyone desires to come after Me, let him deny himself, and take up his cross daily, and follow Me. For whoever desires to save his life will lose it, but whoever loses his life for My sake will save it. For what profit is it to a man if he gains the whole world and is himself destroyed or lost" (**Luke 9:23-25**).

As I have reflected on these words, I have come to understand the practical nature of Jesus' call to discipleship. I must surrender my preferences and agendas and embrace His in order to bear the name disciple. Parenting by taking the path of least resistance, doing what is comfortable, popular, and easy, is certainly convenient. But parenting that builds a legacy requires uncomfortable conversations and mucking through the messiness of emotions and hormones. Parenting that pursues God's will for a child is more time consuming and energy absorbing than simply following popular parenting trends.

It is difficult for me to talk about parenting and grandparenting without using personal illustrations. But let me be clear: Debbie and I struggled and made mistakes. Our lives are a testimony to God's amazing grace, provision, power, and patience for two stumbling, bumbling parents. We give Him glory for helping us get it right more often than we got it wrong.

Investing in the next generation inevitably involves challenging decisions, struggles of will, and uncomfortable conversations. But building godly legacies is never about us. It is about what God does in and through us as we pursue Him daily. God desires to use your life to build a legacy, for your life to be a clear call for your children, grandchildren, co-workers, and friends to follow Christ.

CHAPTER 7

So, What Can We Do?

What can we do to build a legacy that honors God and blesses our children and grandchildren? While there are many principles and truths related to building a spiritual legacy, I will focus on three that have been crucial in my journey.

(1) GO FIRST

The people God uses to influence the next generations are not afraid to provide leadership and establish standards for their families. Having a healthy friendship with your children is important. But your children need a leader who is committed to helping them navigate life in ways that honor God.

The next generations must learn to walk with God, and observing authentic examples is crucial in helping them along the way. When financial institutions train employees to spot counterfeit bills, they do not instruct them to examine fake currency. Instead, they encourage their employees to become so familiar with authentic bills that when they hold a counterfeit, they can immediately notice the difference. In order to prepare the next generations to recognize information and lifestyles that are contrary to God's truth, they must see their parents and grandparents modeling the real thing.

The apostle Paul makes a radical statement in 1 Corinthians 11:1: "Imitate me, just as I also imitate Christ." When placed within the larger context of Paul's messages, we recognize that his desire for others to watch and imitate him had nothing to do with his importance but with the power of God at work in his life. In Philippians 4:13, he affirmed, "I can do all things through Christ who strengthens me." Paul knew from experience that he did not possess the capacity to imitate Christ. But he had great confidence in Christ to do "exceedingly, abundantly above all that we could ask or imagine" (Ephesians 3:20). Paul's role was to surrender his agenda to Christ. The power of the Holy Spirit working in and through him enabled him to be a positive spiritual example for others.

As we "go first" as leaders, we must clearly and consistently model what we want to see God do in our children's lives. And the greatest gift we can give our family is a deep, growing, and powerful walk with Christ. Watching parents and grandparents follow Jesus can dramatically affect children.

My dad was a man's man. A veteran of WWII, he was physically strong with Popeye-type forearms. He worked in the industrial maintenance field, which is a mission field in itself! During my preschool and early elementary years, however, Dad was at best a casual Christian. He was a good man and a loving father, but he was not walking closely with God. He attended church with us each Sunday morning but seldom on Sunday or Wednesday nights. I clearly remember leaving the house to go to church with Mom while Dad sat in his recliner. I am sure I asked Mom why Dad wasn't going with us, because it seemed strange to leave him behind. Then something dramatic happened. Dad had an encounter with Christ that changed everything for all of us. I never remember seeing him sitting in his recliner on Sunday or Wednesday nights again. He was always in the front seat of the car driving Mom and me to church.

Many things changed in our home following Dad's transformation. He "went first" for the rest of his life. Whether during a family prayer time, a worship service, or while teaching a Bible study or sharing his faith in the workplace, Dad set an example of what a deep personal relationship with Christ looked like. Toward the end of his life, Dad's health burdened him in many ways. He spent his final two years in and out of the hospital, but his spirit never wavered. In those days, I spent as much time as possible traveling the three hours home to check on my parents. My life as a pastor limited our face-to-face time, but Dad continued to set a powerful godly example.

On one memorable occasion, Dad was scheduled to be released from the hospital on a Wednesday afternoon. Before I left my office to lead a Bible study and prayer time at the church where I was serving as pastor, I called my parents' house to make sure they had arrived home from the hospital and Dad was okay. No answer! I called the hospital and was told that Dad had indeed been discharged earlier that afternoon. When I returned to my office after the worship time, I continued to call. Around 9:00 p.m., Dad finally answered the phone. I'm sure I sounded like an overprotective parent when I blurted out, "Where have you been?"

"We just got home from choir practice," Dad answered.

Exasperated, I reminded him that he was not healthy and overexerting himself could quickly land him back in a hospital bed. I will never forget his response.

"Son, I had to be with God's people." It was evident that he needed the fellowship of God's people more than anything else at that moment.

As I reflect on that conversation and his words, I still find myself responding today, "Dad, forgive me when I allow feeble excuses to separate me from fellowshipping with my brothers and sisters in Christ. I understand that you required the spiritual nourishment and fellowship more than you needed a comfortable recliner at home."

The generations coming behind us notice our priorities. I became keenly aware of this reality during a Sunday morning worship service at my home church. I was sitting on the front row of the balcony with a view of the floor level of the worship center. As we sang an inspiring worship song, I noticed those directly below me, including a family of five. The son was standing next to his dad, and the two daughters stood on either side of their mom. The daughters sang enthusiastically, just as their mother did. On the other end of the pew, a different story was unfolding. The dad stood with his arms crossed, casually chewing gum and not singing a word. The son looked at his sisters and mother singing joyfully and then at his dad who was totally disengaged. Then he folded his arms and stood solemnly next to his dad, learning by example how to experience a worship service without encountering the Risen Christ.

Let me encourage and challenge you. If you don't find worship to be a joyful, meaningful experience, check your personal relationship with Jesus. Ask Him to give you a fresh vision of who He is and the reality of His presence. Ask Him to give you a heart of worship that is evident to those around you. Show your children and grandchildren what it is like to love the Lord your God with all your heart, soul, mind, and strength. If you can't sing, speak the words of songs to the Lord as an act of worship, allowing the Holy Spirit to refresh you with joy. When the pastor says, "Turn in your Bible," let the next generations see you open your Bible and take out note paper and a pen because you expect to hear a fresh word from the Lord. When you pray aloud with your family, whether over a meal or in corporate worship, let them hear you say more than trite religious clichés. Let there be no doubt you are talking with a holy God whom you know, love, honor, worship, and trust. When a guest visits your church, let your children see you be the first to engage and welcome that person.

Go first. Set the example. Leave spiritual footprints that are easy to follow. Whatever you want to see God do in the next generations of your family, ask Him to do it in your life first.

(2) ENLIST ALLIES

"Be sober; be vigilant; because your adversary the devil walks about like a roaring lion, seeking whom he may devour. Resist him, steadfast in the faith, knowing that the same sufferings are experienced by your brotherhood in the world. But may the God of all grace, who called us to His eternal glory by Christ Jesus, after you have suffered a while, perfect, establish, strengthen, and settle you. To Him be the glory and the dominion forever and ever" (**1 Peter 5:8-11**). Peter's words paint a vivid picture for today's family. These verses came alive for me in a fresh way when my daughters were in elementary school.

In the late 1980s, Debbie and I had an experience of a lifetime: a safari in South Africa. For three days, we rode through Kruger National Park, marveling at the beauty, immensity, and variety of God's creation. Much of what we saw and learned overwhelmed us. During one of the drives, our guide suddenly stopped the car. A herd of impala was grazing quietly in a meadow. The guide explained that a pride of lions was lurking nearby in the tall, wispy grass. Rather than attacking immediately, the lions were quietly sizing up their prey. At the right moment, the leader would signal the attack, singling out the weak and young rather than the strong and swift, thus guaranteeing a successful hunt. Then it hit me: these lions were "walking about, seeking whom [they] may devour." God gives us a similar image in 1 **Peter** of the adversary of our lives, the devil, who is that roaring lion constantly looking for the weak, young, and those who are more easily tempted. He desires to attack families and cause maximum pain and destruction. What can we do as parents and grandparents to push back this assault?

During our child-rearing years, God placed us in wonderful congregations and communities that were filled with parents and grandparents who shared our passion for creating a God-honoring family, people who were intentionally investing in the next generations. We discovered that other adults could speak the same truths into our children's lives that we had, but our daughters often listened more closely to those adults than they did to us. So, we purposefully kept our girls in touch with other spiritually healthy parents and families.

At other times, God brought people into our children's lives, not because of our intentional actions but because

He loved them and had a purpose for them that was beyond anything we could ask or imagine. Even when we were unaware of the challenges they were facing or how best to pray for them, God honored our prayers by using other people, specific circumstances, and the Holy Spirit's powerful work to guide and protect them. Now we are asking Him to do the same for our grandchildren.

Some key people God used (and is still using) in our girls' lives were in Debbie's small prayer group. While this group prayed about many things, perhaps their greatest calling was to pray for their children and grandchildren.

FROM DEBBIE

Being the pastor's kids, our children were blessed to have many people praying for them. I knew as a mother that I could ask many people to pray specifically for our girls. We are grateful to have been members of churches that made intentional efforts to pray for the next generations. One of the special blessings over the past 20 or more years has been a small group of ladies whose original purpose was to pray for me as their pastor's wife. Each person felt a personal calling to this prayer relationship and even though we no longer serve in that congregation, this small group has "reared" our children through prayer, and now we do so with our grandchildren.

A special moment God gave our family through these allies was a "shower of blessing" over our daughters before they got married. Many of our friends joined to compile a book of practical advice concerning marriage and prayers of blessing for each daughter and her fiancé. This book was presented to the couple during a time of fellowship in a friend's home, and the gathering concluded with everyone encircling the engaged couple and speaking prayers of blessing over their lives, marriage, and home. In recent years, we have had the privilege of hosting these "showers of blessing" in our home for our friends' children.

As we pray together with like-minded Christian friends, God reveals His heart for our children, encourages us, and makes us sensitive to how He desires to use us in each child's life. More recently, I have been a member of a small group at my home church. One night as we gathered, I was burdened for one of my grandchildren but could not voice the details and need due to laryngitis. As we began our prayer time, the group members started to pray for my grandchild without knowing my burden. It was so incredible to me that God placed him on their hearts that night.

I see a significant challenge in the body of Christ today. Christians seem hesitant to enlist allies for their children. They build silos of isolation rather than relationships, often relating at a superficial level rather than speaking deeply into each other's lives, sharing specific joys, sorrows, struggles, victories, and wisdom with fellow believers. This isolation separates them from the herd and gives Satan an opening to wound or devour families.

When I was a child, my parents' church friends shared a common commitment to see their children walk upright lives. Many times, one of my parents' friends would correct me, and I knew without a doubt whom my parents would believe when getting to the bottom of the situation! I was surrounded by a village in the best sense of that word. I fear we are so busy today with our personal agendas and schedules that we have little margin in our lives to build meaningful relationships with other parents and their children. Without investing in each other's lives, we unwittingly leave our kids without the protection of the spiritual village.

Pride is another subtle but powerful force that disengages families from the Christian community's life-giving support. While serving as a pastor, I had many conversations in my office with distraught, discouraged, angry, bewildered parents who were struggling with their child's attitudes and choices. After listening to their concerns, my first question was always, "Who is praying with you for your child?"

To my surprise, the answer was often, "No one. We don't want anyone to know about this, because we would be too embarrassed."

I would reply, "So, what you're saying is that maintaining your reputation is more important than having others cry out to God on your family's behalf?" I was not asking these parents to announce their family's struggles in the church newsletter but to ask the Heavenly Father to place on their heart fellow believers who could join them in specific petition and intercession.

Thankfully, these conversations compelled many of these parents to enlist others to pray for their children and to pray for their friends' children in return. In fact, the prayer ministry at a church I pastored in South Carolina even developed a prayer group for parents and grandparents of prodigal children. This group met weekly to share, pray, and encourage one another as they sought to see their family members return to the Lord.

My friend and colleague Richard Blackaby shared this experience:

> While I was the president of a theological seminary, I used to meet in my office regularly with six male students. We would discuss issues related to leadership as well as what it meant to develop into a man of God. At the close of one session, I asked if I could share with them a prayer request. One of my teenage sons was going through a very difficult time in his life. I was concerned about him. Most of the students in the meeting attended our church and knew my son. I told them that my wife and I needed all the help we could get with our son and that if they ever had a chance to speak a word of encouragement to him when they saw him at church, I would be deeply grateful.

As we were dismissing our meeting, several of the students lingered behind. They said to me, "We can't believe what you just did. You are the president of this school and a highly respected leader. Yet, you just confessed to us students that you were struggling with one of your kids, and you asked us for our help. We just can't believe you would be so candid with a bunch of students like us."

I thought about what they said and then replied, "You have to understand something. I love my son very much. Nothing is more important to me right now than seeing him overcome what he is facing. If I thought it would help to climb on top of my house and shout from the rooftop that I needed help for my son, I'd do it in a heartbeat. You see, I never want my pride to stand in the way of getting help for my kids." I have known too many parents who were more concerned about what others would think if they knew about the problems they had with their kids than they were about getting help for those kids. I wasn't going to be one of those parents.

Culture sets us up for struggles by holding up a model of success so anything that falls short of that perfect standard is considered failure. Rather than risk our image in the community or church, we closet our children's failures and trumpet their successes. We all want to succeed, but the reality is that we might not. Without God's grace, we are doomed to fail as parents and grandparents. God often dispenses His grace in the form of a fellow believer who comes alongside our family at just the right time, perhaps for only a specific moment or season. We know that it is God who will "perfect, establish, strengthen and settle" us, but what a blessing when He chooses to act through fellow Christians.

Debbie and I wanted our children to love having their friends in our home, so we offered to host church, school, or friend gatherings, whether planned or spontaneous. Doing so sometimes meant changing our plans or staying up later than we wanted, but we never regretted knowing where our children were and whom they were with! Making your home a place of fun, joy, and spontaneity encourages your children to bring their friends home with them. Of course, it helps if Mom is the best cook in town! While I am sure we embarrassed our girls on numerous occasions, whether on purpose or accidentally, we were delighted and thankful to welcome their friends into our home on many occasions. As a result, God gave us lots of children to love and encourage.

In **Ephesians 2:19-22**, Paul offers a powerful and inspiring description of the body of Christ: "Now, therefore, we are no longer strangers and foreigners, but fellow citizens with the saints and members of the household of God, having been built on the foundation of the apostles and prophets, Jesus Christ Himself being the chief cornerstone, in whom the whole building, being fitted together, grows into a holy temple in the Lord, in whom you also are being built together for a dwelling place of God in the Spirit." Immerse yourself in the fellowship of the Church and enlist allies for the sake of the generations to come. Could I encourage you to allow God to help you jettison your pride and actively seek allies as you influence the next generations? What adjustments do you need to make to surround your children with godly influences?

(3) FOCUS ON WHAT MATTERS

Hills have played an important role in military history. Taking and holding a strategically placed hill allows soldiers to fight from a position of strength. A high vantage point also gives military leaders the advantage of detecting advances and vulnerabilities in the enemy below. The more strategically placed the hill, the higher the price leaders are willing to pay to conquer it. Not every hill is worth the sacrifice, but sometimes circumstances demand paying whatever price is necessary to ascend and control the high ground. Whoever holds that pivotal position often wins the battle.

In family relationships, especially between parents and children, certain crucial moments can determine the direction the child or family will take for months and years to come. Conversations about choosing friends, family guidelines, and appropriate disciplines carry various weight depending on how they affect those involved. Sometimes parents correctly assess the hill's value, and sometimes our scales are out of balance in ridiculous, occasionally laughable ways.

Though I was proud of my girls in so many ways, certain hills caused me continual angst. For the oldest, it was the cleanliness of her room. In fact, I was certain that small creatures lived inside, convinced we would never find them amongst the rubble. For the youngest, it was her casual attitude toward academics, as though studying were an option, not a necessity. Both issues flew in the face of my understanding of appropriate priorities. After all, "cleanliness is next to godliness" and we are to "study to show [ourselves] approved." Perhaps I was guilty of either re-writing Scripture or taking it out of context. But sometimes we can become so passionate about an issue that we lose touch with sound reasoning, especially when we turn a passing stage of life into a mountain we erroneously believe will determine our children's eternal destiny!

My continual harping on these issues created a communication gap between the girls and me. I am certain they could sense when one of my rants was imminent and found creative ways to be inconspicuously absent or simply tolerated me until I finished. One morning as I was praying, I asked God to show me if there were any areas in my life that needed adjustment. As Richard Blackaby says, "When you ask God a question, you have to be prepared for the answer." Immediately, I felt the Spirit put a finger on my preachy attitudes toward my daughters.

"But God, I am trying to help them keep their priorities in order," I said.

God responded, "Okay, so if they have clean rooms and good grades but are no longer interested in your opinion on important matters, what have you accomplished? Are you willing to sacrifice lifelong influence for a temporary victory?"

At that moment, I surrendered my agenda for my daughters and asked God to help me recognize which hills really mattered. That ugly pontification monster reared its head in my spirit many times, but I asked God to set a guard over my mouth, and to this day I am grateful He adjusted my vision of what was really important!

As I mentioned before, pop culture exerts a tremendous influence on families. With a plethora of information only a click away, we have become well versed in sports, business, economics, travel, food, fashion, politics, and the list goes on and on. No subject matter seems inaccessible to us. An inherent danger with the constant flood of information directed at us is that we struggle to turn down the volume and focus on God's voice. I have found He has much to speak into our lives if we "park our hearts" and remain still in His presence.

Perhaps a brief pop quiz will help you ascertain whether you are focusing on what matters. Get a pen and paper, and here we go! If I asked you to write for 10 minutes about your favorite sports team, recipe, or a recent news event, could you easily fill the time? What if I then challenged you to write for 10 minutes about a Scripture passage God has been using to speak into your life lately? Could you share the truths He has revealed and how they are influencing your decisions and relationships? The words on the paper in front of you reveal your priorities.

It is impossible to embrace the priorities of a fallen culture and keep our minds and hearts focused on God at the same time. Anything we run to for comfort, security, or meaning besides Him is an idol. And sooner or later, God will declare war on our idols. We must be careful when developing attachments to temporary things, for they intoxicate our soul. For much of my life, I suffered from allergies that caused violent sneezing attacks and made my eyes swell. One medicine that alleviated my symptoms was Benadryl. But relief came with a price: a drowsiness that made me feel as though someone dropped a weight on my eyelids. My reflexes slowed, and sooner or later a nap was in order!

The noise of daily life often acts like Benadryl to our soul, making us slow to hear and follow God's leadership and instructions. I like Corrie ten Boom's advice: "Hold everything in your hands lightly, otherwise it hurts when God pries your fingers open." Be careful about attaching meaning and purpose in your life to temporary things that will produce great pain when God severs the connection.

Let the next generations watch you follow Christ, even when doing so is countercultural. Even when it is diametrically opposed to what your children or grandchildren want. Two incidents stand out in my memory. I got one right and the other wrong. Let's begin with the success. Several decades ago, when my girls were in elementary school, God clearly opened the door for me to leave Atlanta and move to South Carolina to become the pastor of Pickens First Baptist Church. The girls were well settled into our church and community. Atlanta was a burgeoning city, while Pickens was a small county seat town. When I told the girls what God had called me to do, they struggled to wrap their minds around such a drastic change. They couldn't imagine any benefits of living in a small town versus the largest metropolis in the South. Why leave security for uncertainty? But parenting is about going first and focusing on what matters, even when our children don't understand.

Shortly before announcing our plans to our Atlanta congregation, we gathered as a family in the master bedroom of our house. Crying, our oldest daughter, Jamie, prayed, "God, I don't want to leave Atlanta, but I know you have called my daddy, so I will go."

In that moment, I experienced confusing emotions. I remember praying, "God, as we follow You, I am once again entrusting my family to you. Please shape our hearts to be like Yours."

God used the subsequent 18 years I served as a pastor in South Carolina to do exceedingly abundantly more than we could have ever asked or imagined (**Ephesians 3:20**). Both girls thrived in many ways, but perhaps the greatest blessing was seeing how God shaped them as His children.

Almost 25 years after the bedroom prayer time in Atlanta, Jamie, a youth leader at her church, wrote these words to Debbie and me: "I wanted to say thank you this morning for the godly example you have always been in following God's will in your ministry, even if it didn't make sense to Betsy and me or to those around you. Because I have experienced that in our home, this morning, through the leading of the Holy Spirit, I was able to lead a prayer for our student minister and his family as they are preparing today to tell people they have taken a position at another church. Thank you for always showing us what it means to be faithful to God's sovereign plan. I know I am not always easy to deal with, but the lessons you have lived out for me have stuck, and I am appreciative of them."

Connecting God's activity to life events is one of the greatest gifts you can give your children and grandchildren. Our decision to leave Atlanta for Pickens was not based on best available options, finances, houses, etc. Instead, we acted based on our personal commitment to follow God's leadership. Thus, we prayed for wisdom in how best to live out our calling, knowing we could trust God's provision.

My most powerful memory of getting it wrong occurred in Germany. My family had accompanied me on a group trip I was leading to attend the Passion Play in Oberammergau. With my Type A personality dulling my senses to anything besides my own agenda, my youngest daughter, Betsy, approached me with an innocent question. My self-centered response was like a spear going right to her heart. While Jamie accompanied me on the second leg of the trip, Betsy and Debbie were scheduled to head home earlier with the rest of the group.

After returning home, Betsy headed to college, but I could not get over the knot in the pit of my stomach that gnawed at me daily. One morning during my devotion time, God put His finger squarely on the knot and pushed hard. I was out of fellowship with Him and unable to hear from Him because I had sinned against my daughter (and God) with my unkind words. I called her and asked what she was doing for lunch that day. When she indicated that she didn't have plans, I told her that she was having lunch with me. I remember driving those two hours to her college town with tears running down my face as I asked God to give me a spirit of humility. I looked into Betsy's eyes and told her how sorry I was, asked her to forgive me, and received the precious gift of God's grace and my daughter's forgiveness.

God's grace is available to anyone who seeks forgiveness, not just from God but from those who were offended. Ask God if there is anything in your relationships that requires confessing, addressing, and forgiving. Too many families walk through life with wounds in their hearts that God is ready and willing to mend. Don't let pride make your family vulnerable to the one who is seeking to devour them. Ask God to help you make the necessary adjustments in your life so you can focus on what really matters!

CHAPTER 8

Practical Spiritual Priorities

In His Word, God reveals many things that are on His heart for our families. But I see two clear priorities He gives to parents and grandparents who long to see the next generations of their family follow Him.

(1) TEACH THEM THE WORD OF GOD

As I shared earlier, **Deuteronomy 6:4-7** speaks to the importance of sharing God's Word with the next generations: "Hear, O Israel: The Lord our God, the Lord is one! You shall love the Lord your God with all your heart, with all your soul, and with all your strength. And these words which I command you today shall be in your heart. You shall teach them diligently to your children and shall talk of them when you sit in your house, when you walk by the way, when you lie down, and when you rise up." When coupled with God's words to the spiritual leader of the home in **Ephesians 6:4**, Scripture offers a vivid picture of accountability to God for living out what He desires for our children.

One of the best ways to "provoke your children" is to leave them to face problems, decisions, and relationships without first instilling the plumb line of God's truth in their lives. When we fail to invest God's truth in their lives, we leave them to face life's great questions on their own. As I mentioned earlier, surveys reveal that 66% of those who attend church regularly while growing up will walk away from their faith after entering college. I believe one reason young people are leaving the faith is the disconnect they observe between what they hear at church and how their parents live at home. Merely taking our children to church will not persuade them to know, trust, and follow God. But living out God's truths before them each day in our home will have a lasting influence on their life and serve as a reference point for future decisions.

Parents, it is impossible to pass along to our children something that does not exist in us. We must personally pursue the truth of God's Word daily, asking the Holy Spirit to transform our thinking and equip us with eternal truth. We must also ask for discernment concerning when and how to speak and live out God's truth before our children.

In **Colossians 2:6-10**, the apostle Paul offers both encouragement and a warning concerning the crucial need to know and walk in truth: "As you therefore have received Christ Jesus the Lord, so walk in Him, rooted and built up in Him and established in the faith, as you have been taught, abounding in it with thanksgiving. Beware lest anyone cheat you through philosophy and empty deceit, according to the tradition of men, according to the basic principles of the world, and not according to Christ. For in Him dwells all the fullness of the Godhead bodily; and you are complete in Him, who is the head of all principality and power." It is imperative that we pursue a deepening relationship with Christ so we can offer our children a clear picture of faithful and God-centered living. They must see us pushing back against the "tradition of men" and passionately pursuing all that it means to "walk in Him."

Consider the opportunities you have each day to invest in your child. What influences will you allow to shape your child's mind, spirit, ethics, and worldview? When you consider God's words in Deuteronomy and Ephesians, you may realize you need to restructure your family's priorities, schedules, and media boundaries to create an atmosphere that is conducive to God's truth in your home.

Since becoming grandparents, Debbie and I have asked God to make us sensitive to practical ways we can join His activity in each of our grandchildren's lives. We do not ask God for permission to preach a sermon to the next generation. Rather, we strive to build relationships that naturally lead to conversations about eternal truth. While God will make you sensitive to the children's needs and the ways you can establish a meaningful relationship with each one, here are some channels that have been effective for us.

Ask God to help you discover connection points with each child. Every child is different, but they are all important to God. We must ask God to make us sensitive to specific ways we can connect with each child. For my oldest grandson, Thomas, one of those connections has been through classic television programs such as *The Andy Griffith Show*. Since it is one of my favorite shows, Thomas and I watched it together often in his early years. As Debbie and I sensed that he was getting hooked, we purchased a trivia game based on the show. We have been playing that game for several years now, and he recently celebrated his sixth consecutive win over Papa! This common interest has led to conversations about other subjects as well (that just might be more eternal than Barney's hilarious attempts to catch a crook).

Pray for teachable moments. Ask God to allow you to use current situations, conversations, and decisions to turn your child's attention toward God's truth and how it relates to daily choices, priorities, behavior, thoughts, attitudes, and relationships. Each day pray for the Holy Spirit to grant you sensitivity to others, especially your children and grandchildren. I pray a specific prayer every day: "Father, allow me to see the people I encounter today the way you see them; allow me to hear their words the way you hear them; help me to respond to each person in a manner that would honor you."

During my devotion time one morning when Thomas (who was 10 years old at the time) was visiting the farm where Debbie and I live, God pressed into me the truths of **Ephesians 4:29**: "Let no corrupt word proceed out of your mouth, but what is good for necessary edification, that it may impart grace to the hearers." The Holy Spirit reminded me that I need to ask God to set a guard over my words, think before I speak, and ask myself, "Will these words impart grace to others?"

Later that day, I was walking on the farm while Thomas rode his bike beside me. My mom was out walking as well. As Thomas and I passed her, she asked, "Don't you need a jacket?"

My first thought was, "I'm a grown man who is capable of determining when I need a jacket!" But **Ephesians 4:29** leapt to the front of my mind, and I responded, "No, thanks. I'm good!"

As we moved on, Thomas said, "Your mom sure does love you."

"Yes, she does," I responded.

After a few moments of silence, he said, "I wish I could be more like that with my mom. Sometimes I argue with her."

I realized at that moment God had given me **Ephesians 4:29** not only for my benefit but for my grandson's as well. I responded, "Let me tell you about a Scripture

God used in my life this morning. . ." and I shared the verse and its application for relationships, especially in a family.

After another period of silence, Thomas said, "Papa, I always like coming to the farm."

"I'm glad you do!"

"When I come here, I always get a spiritual truth," he said.

His words were powerful, and my first thought was that my grandchildren are always listening. My second thought was how often I miss the opportunity to invest spiritual truth into my family's lives. My final thought and prayer was, "God, help me never miss an opportunity again."

Later that day, I gave Thomas an index card with the text of **Ephesians 4:29** written on it so he could place it beside his bed or on his dresser as a reminder to be careful of his words.

Ephesians 4:29 should be set as a banner above every aspect of our lives as leaders and influencers of the next generations. Even when correcting a child, use words that can build up (by providing correction and instruction) and bring grace (a sense that the child has worth and the capacity to get it right next time). Too often, I hear parents correcting their children, and while their correction is likely on target, their tone of voice and word choice are bitter and wounding. My concern is these children could turn away from God and the Church when they hit the collegiate years. Having the freedom to choose their beliefs, they often turn to other sources to define their self-worth with many of their choices bringing pain and tragedy to their life and family. While the parent may have spoken truth, the result was an embittered, resentful child.

Be intentional. Children are born with curiosity and a desire to learn, and they will satisfy that need in many ways: in the classroom, on the playground, at church, and in the home. Scripture passages such as **Deuteronomy 6** and **Ephesians 6** remind us that the values that honor God are best learned at home. And teaching requires intentionality, planning, and commitment. One way we have been intentionally teaching our grandchildren is through a Bible study Debbie wrote. The study focuses on basic truths for believers—the attributes of God, the Persons of Jesus and the Holy Spirit, and the significance of the Bible and prayer. On a smaller scale, we select a memory verse for our annual family beach week that we memorize and repeat several times each day, taking time to discuss the truths in the verse and how they apply to our lives.

Hebrews 4:12 tells us that "the Word of God is living and powerful," and Paul reminds us in **2 Timothy 3:16** that Scripture "is profitable for doctrine, for reproof, for correction, for instruction in righteousness." Ask God to set His Word as the banner over your life as a parent and grandparent, to use you to bring His Word to bear on the lives of your children and grandchildren. I pray that God's Word will be "a lamp to your feet and a light to your path," and the next generations will benefit from the glow.

One of my greatest desires is to leave a legacy of loving God's Word that will encourage my children and grandchildren to love and cherish God's Word as well. I will share a few of the things I have done or am still doing toward that end.

When my children were babies, and even into older childhood, I would sing the same collection of hymns to them as I rocked them before bed. I have continued this tradition with each of my grandchildren. The greatest thrill has been when they are about two years old, and they begin to sing with me! I remember one specific occasion when, late at night, one of our grandsons, Jase, was hallucinating because of a high fever. With my son-in-law out of town, my daughter Betsy called our house, and I rushed to help her with Jase and her two other children. As I held Jase close while he screamed out in fear, I began to sing the songs we had sung together all his life. In a few moments, I heard a little voice begin singing with me, and his body grew calm and the fears disappeared. Then he said, "That was good, Gran. Let's sing again."

Joshua 22:5 is a life prayer for my children and grandchildren, especially the words, "to love the Lord your God, to walk in all His ways, to keep His commandments, to hold fast to Him, and to serve

Him with all your heart and with all your soul." I set that verse to the tune of a familiar hymn, and I sing it over my grandchildren when I rock them or as I rub their back while they drift off to sleep. Sometimes they sing it with me, which gives me hope that the Holy Spirit will enable them to remember the Scripture Gran prayed over them. Recently, at Christmas, I gave each grandchild a framed copy of "Gran's Prayer." Thomas, almost 14 at that time, immediately said, "This is what you used to sing to me!"

To help each child memorize Scripture, we have used games, songs, and alphabet verses (a verse for each letter). It is amazing how God has gifted children to learn and memorize. When Gray, our youngest grandson, was 2 years old, I decided to quote John 3:16 to him every time I rocked him. Before long, he could say the verse from memory. By putting Scripture cards in their lunch boxes, sticky notes with Scriptures on their mirrors, and now texting Scripture to my oldest grandsons, I continue to keep God's Word in front of them. Sometimes I share a truth from my daily quiet time with my adult children via email or text.

My greatest endeavor has been writing a Bible study for my grandchildren. I was burdened by the statistics of young people leaving the faith. I wondered if they were leaving because they don't really know and love God personally but have instead been relying on their parents' faith. I wanted to do my part in helping my grandchildren know the nature and promises of God well through Scripture. My desire is that they would grow deeply in love with Him and serve Him all their lives.

(2) BE A PRAYER WARRIOR FOR YOUR FAMILY

FROM DEBBIE

As a grandmother of five young children, I have occasionally kept them overnight or for several days. During those times, I am reminded of the challenges young mothers face in having personal quiet time with the Lord. No matter how carefully a mother plans to get up early or use nap time to read her Bible and pray, a child will inevitably wake up at dawn, get sick, or decide not to go to sleep for a nap. Countless interruptions and changes of plan can happen with young children. Just coping with the daily demands and lack of sleep are challenges enough!

When I was a mother with young children, a dear friend and mentor who was on staff at the church my husband served encouraged me many times. She had six grown children and told me how, at times, it was impossible to have a personal quiet time. She encouraged me not to feel guilty but to acknowledge that it was a season, cherish mothering young children, and find practical ways to keep focused on the Lord other than spending large segments of time reading my Bible and praying. She assured me the day of focused quiet time with the Lord would come again!

One thing I found to be important was designating a "quiet time place" for the moments I could be alone with the Lord. This space was equipped with my Bible, a journal, and devotional books. Even as young children, my daughters knew this area was my special place with the Lord. Other lessons I learned were to turn everyday activities into prayer prompts for my children, such as folding their clothes and asking God to clothe them in His righteousness, making their beds and asking God to guard their thoughts and dreams and calm their fears at night, and picking up their shoes and praying for God to guard their feet, the steps they take, and the places they go.

Other suggestions I have found helpful are to write a verse on an index card and keep it in a visible place as a reminder of God's attributes or promises. Some days may be so intense that just a glance at God's Word is encouraging! Put Scriptures on sticky notes on your bathroom mirror as reminders to pray for yourself and your family. Memorize them with your children. Change them out weekly to keep your worship and prayers fresh. Keep a Bible or devotional book in your car (or download a daily devotional app) to read while waiting to pick a child up from school or extra-curricular activities. Keep a *Daily Light*[1] book of Scriptures on the kitchen counter to read when you have a few spare minutes or read it aloud to your family while they're eating breakfast or supper. Trade out childcare for a few hours periodically with another mother so you both can have a "mini retreat with the Lord" instead of shopping, going to appointments, or doing housework. Make Scripture cards to take with you on a walk to use as prompts in your prayer time. Keep worship music playing continuously in your home and car. These are just a few suggestions, but the principle is to combine desire and intentionality with creativity. It is possible to embrace motherhood with a worshipful heart!

The belief that God has the capacity to do anything at any time for anyone energizes prayer warriors. As a pastor, I often stood before the congregation with new parents as they dedicated their children to God. When we dedicate children, we indicate our desire for our homes to be a place where God is honored, and we commit to rear our children in an environment that introduces them to God and His love for them as expressed through Jesus. We enter into a covenant with God to join Him in developing a spiritual legacy in our family. But let me encourage you—don't simply dedicate your children to the Lord at birth. Rather, bring your children before the Lord each day, re-commit them into His hands, and re-commit yourself as their parents.

Jennifer Kennedy Dean shares this powerful picture of prayer for our children and grandchildren:

> By saturating our children's lives in prayer, we activate God's will in every realm of their lives. Prayer has no limits—no time limits, no geographical limits. Just as surely as we can provide for our children's present and daily needs through prayer, we can also reach into their futures, laying a foundation of blessings for our children, our grandchildren and all of our descendants ... we can leave behind for our descendants a spiritual trust that can never be stolen, squandered or lost.[2]

If we long to leave a legacy of prayer and a love for God's Word that will reach far into future generations, we will nurture our children and grandchildren in the atmosphere of prayer. When Debbie saw the "Whoever Wants the Next Generation Will Get Them" sign at the church in Brevard, NC, she said the statement so gripped her heart she determined that on her watch of prayer "no one will want my grandchildren more than I want them to belong to Christ. I realized that it is going to take more than 'bless them and keep them safe' prayers. It must be intentional, specific, and strategic prayer founded in the Word of God, the kind of prayer that takes sacrifices of time, effort, and energy. It must be the kind of prayer Paul describes in **Ephesians 6** that confronts 'the powers and world forces of darkness and spiritual forces of evil in the heavenly places.'"

SCRIPTURE PRAYERS AND JOURNALING

FROM DEBBIE

When my girls were born, I knew praying for them was important, even though I'm not sure I fully understood why. But as I have grown deeper in my prayer life, I realize the truth of **James 5:16**, that my prayers are powerful and effective in activating God's power, purposes, provisions, and will in specific ways. My prayers will make a difference in the future generations even after I am gone.

The most powerful tool we have in praying for our children is the Word of God, because it is living, active, and reflects God's heart, desires, and will. He promised in **Isaiah 55:11** that His Word will not return to Him void without accomplishing the purpose for which He sent it. I have found there are many ways to pray Scripture over our children:

- Allow daily activities to prompt specific Scripture prayers:
  - When picking up shoes, we can ask God to establish their footsteps in His Word (**Psalm 119:133**).
  - When holding a child's hand, we can pray that her hands would serve God and others (**Proverbs 31:20, Colossians 3:23**).
  - When seeing a Bible in a child's room, we can pray that he would treasure

God's Word, hiding it in his heart (**Psalm 119:11**).

- Use Scripture passages to pray for godly character, such as praying specific fruits of the spirit would be manifested in their lives (**Galatians 5:22-23**).
- Choose a Scripture prayer focus in January to pray over our children throughout the year.
- Ask God to show us Scriptures to pray at specific times. One day as I asked God how to pray for my teenage grandson concerning some challenges he was facing, I read God's instructions to Moses in **Exodus 19:4** to tell the Israelites, "I bore you up on eagle's wings and brought you to Myself." My heart responded, "Lord, bear Thomas up on eagle's wings and bring him to Yourself."

Journaling prayers for my children and grandchildren is very important to me, because this practice gives me written records of my encounters with God on their behalf. In the Old Testament, God repeatedly revealed Himself to His people, but they kept forgetting and going back to their own ways. I don't ever want to forget what God has done, said, or shown me to pray for my children and grandchildren, and I don't want them to forget either.

Journaling can deepen our faith, because it provides a clear record of how God has initiated and responded to our prayers, allowing us to be a part of His work. I remember feeling impressed on February 29 (leap year) to pray for my grandson, Ashley, and his salvation. The next day, he called to tell me he had given his life to Christ at an after-school Bible club meeting. One year later, I texted my daughter Jamie so she could remind Ashley that it was the anniversary of the day he accepted Christ. He challenged the date, but his parents told him it was useless to argue with Gran and her prayer journal!

Seeing the record of God's response to our prayers motivates us to persevere in prayer, especially in troubling times or when praying for prodigal children. Several of my friends have retained hope in praying for their prodigal child, because they have written records of their prayers, God's promises from Scripture, and glimpses of hope they can return to for encouragement to wait and watch expectantly, believing that the end of the story has yet to be told.

Journaling can also become a written legacy of prayer to pass on to our children and grandchildren. **Psalm 102:18** states, "This will be written for the generation to come, that a people yet to be created may praise the Lord." I keep a prayer journal for each of my children and grandchildren to record

Scriptures, prayers, and ways I see God working in their lives. I plan to give their journals to them one day so they can know how God has worked in their lives through prayer.

Praying for our family daily is the greatest and most precious gift we can give them. But it is an investment of time and energy that is sometimes challenging and painful. However, when God knows our hearts are devoted to praying for our children, He reveals specific issues or situations they are facing so we can go into battle on their behalf by praying His Word over them and sometimes even fasting.

When Debbie and I had young children (and now grandchildren), we were willing to do whatever was needed to help them succeed. Most parents would willingly lay down their lives for their family. But are you willing to make the necessary sacrifices to invest in their future through prayer so they can live under God's purposes and blessings? Are you a person of prayer? Corrie ten Boom asked this poignant question: "Is prayer your steering wheel or your spare tire?"

Two truths about what God does in our lives when we pray are critically important to understand.

GOD SHAPES OUR HEART TO BE LIKE HIS HEART

Communication deepens relationships, including our relationship with God. **Jeremiah 29:11** reveals God's heart for us and our families: "'For I know the thoughts I think toward you,' says the Lord, 'thoughts of peace and not of evil, to give you a future and a hope.'" And God promises to reveal His thoughts to us in **Jeremiah 33:3**, "Call to me and I will answer you and show you great and mighty things which you do not know." However, as Henry Blackaby has often stated, God's revelation to us occurs best when we set aside unhurried time to be still before Him.

With the plethora of activities available to families today, personal prayer time often resembles a NASCAR pit stop. We race around the seemingly endless circle of daily living, pull into our devotion time, and ask God to meet our needs, hear our petitions, fill us with spiritual truth, and make all the necessary heart adjustments, and to do it quickly because we must get back in the race. In my experience, God prefers a "parked heart" to a heart that is distracted by a fast-paced life. I have felt God's truth affect me deeply when I have chosen to be still before Him. For me, prayer time is not as much about telling God what is on my mind as it is about asking Him to speak to me and adjust my thinking and priorities for my family to match His will. Richard Foster encourages us to "wait on God. Wait, silent and still. Wait, attentive and responsive. Learn that trust precedes faith."[3]

One challenge we face in hearing from God is that our devotion time is often focused on God's hand rather than His face. What do I mean? In Scripture, God's face represents His character, and His hand represents His activity. It is a great temptation to be primarily an "asker" when we pray. While God invites us to bring our desires, struggles, and questions to Him, experience has taught me that He is more interested in developing my character. After He establishes His truth and passions in my thinking, He will help me navigate the issues I am facing in my home, church, or workplace. Daniel Henderson states, "I have learned that if all we ever do is seek God's hand, we may miss His face; but if we seek His face, He will be glad to open His hand and satisfy the deepest desires of our hearts."[4] Could it be that I have often missed God's truth for life decisions and circumstances because I have been more focused on things than on His character and purposes for me and my family?

At the time of this writing, Debbie and I have been married for more than 40 years. We know much more about each other today than we did in the early years of our relationship. I can attest from personal experience that some things are better learned over time. The longer we have known each other, the more deeply I can relate to my wife, the more fully I trust her, and the more content I am merely being in her presence. Some evenings, simply sitting near her is enough to still my spirit and bring me peace after a hectic day.

God invites us to live in a love relationship with Him. The conversation God offers through prayer is the heart of this relationship. As we communicate with Him, experiencing His presence and becoming sensitive to what is on His heart, we are profoundly changed. While the answers I have received to my prayers are wonderful, the deepening of my trust, confidence, and contentment in my Heavenly Father has affected me even more deeply. David's words in **Psalm 27:8** speak to this truth: "When You said, 'Seek My face,' my heart said to You, 'Your face, Lord, I will seek.'" The time we spend before the Lord's face greatly increases our effectiveness as influencers of the next generations.

Scripture should play a significant role in deepening our prayer life and shaping us so we more fully reflect God's character. In **John 15:7-8**, Jesus promises, "If you abide in Me, and My words abide in you, you will ask what you desire, and it shall be done for you. By this My Father is glorified, that you bear much fruit; so you will be My disciples." Jesus teaches that the fruit of our lives is directly correlated to the depth and intimacy of our relationship with the Word of God. He zeroes in on the character of abiding, parking our hearts before Him and His Word. When we abide in Christ, the Holy Spirit uses the truth of God's Word to align our prayers with God's will so He is pleased to respond to them. Allow God's Word to shape the way you pray for your children and grandchildren. You can have confidence that He will respond!

PRAYER ENABLES US TO JOIN GOD'S ACTIVITY IN OUR FAMILY

As we open ourselves to God when we pray, being still and learning to recognize His voice, He will not only shape our hearts to be more God-centered, but He will also call us to join Him in what He is doing and wants to do in and through our families. As we become sensitive to God's activity in our children's and grandchildren's lives, we are better equipped to pray for them.

Daniel Henderson states, "One of the great results of transforming prayer is that people recognize God at work because they have joined Him in that work through their prayers. Their hearts are sensitized to His presence, His power, and His purposes."[5] In prayer, God refines our thinking and our senses so we can know when to write a note, send an email, or take advantage of teachable moments with our children and grandchildren.

God used a crossroads moment in our family to teach me the importance of praying and seeking His heart for my children. Betsy had graduated from college and moved home to begin her career. The living arrangement was temporary, as she was engaged to be married the following summer. For several reasons, we did not feel that her relationship honored God, and we believed the marriage would be a mistake. The one challenge, and a large one, was that Betsy was an adult and had not asked for our opinion.

As I began to pray for Betsy and this relationship, God showed me truths from Scripture that related directly to the situation. I wrote down verses and truths for several weeks as God faithfully responded to my prayers. In a moment of impatience and frustration, I reminded God that He could simply cut me out as the middleman and speak these truths directly to my daughter. His response was powerful and life-altering: she was not yet ready to hear His truth!

The wedding date grew closer, and the invitations were lying on our kitchen counter. One morning as I prayed for Betsy, I determined that before the day ended, I must tell her what God had revealed to me, even if doing so cost me a relationship I cherished. That evening as I was sitting in my recliner, I heard the front door open, and she entered the room. In a way only a daughter could, she said, "Dad, put down your popcorn. I'm going to sit in this chair and ask you some questions, and you better tell me the truth!" For the next 30 minutes, I had the privilege of sharing God's heart and truth with her. While God had been revealing His thoughts to me about my daughter, He had also been working in her life. Several weeks later, she called off the wedding. Today, Betsy is married to a godly man and they have three of our precious grandchildren.

God taught me so much during those days and in the time since. Here are a few lessons I learned as I reflected on all God was doing and the practical impact His activity had on my life.

God is always at work in and around us. As I prayed for Betsy, God used my time before Him not only to reveal His truth for her but also to prepare my heart to share those truths with her when she was ready to listen. In the den that evening, He gave us a common desire to hear from Him and know His heart for the situation.

Parents and grandparents must seek God's heart for their children and grandchildren. There will be crucial moments in our children's and grandchildren's lives when they will need a word from God. In those moments, they must hear more than our best thinking. We must seek God daily, because our best thoughts can have little effect, but the power of God's truth can penetrate the heart.

God desires to bless us in ways that are beyond what we could ask or imagine. The truths of **Matthew 7:11** affected me in powerful ways as I reflected on our conversation. Jesus said, "If you then, being evil, know how to give good gifts to your children, how much more will your Father who is in heaven give good things to those who ask Him!" My desire to bless my daughter and share God's truth with her was so powerful that, at times, I felt I would explode. If I experienced that desire so strongly in my sinful nature, how much more does the perfect Father in heaven desire to share His truth with each of His children? How often do we fail to enjoy all God has for us because we refuse to be still and hear from Him? How many times have I robbed my children or grandchildren of God's best gifts because I was too busy to wait patiently for God's response to my prayers?

There is wisdom for life decisions that we only receive through prayer. A final picture I carry with me is a deeper understanding of **Jeremiah 33:3**: "Call to me, and I will answer you, and show you great and mighty things, which you do not know." We don't have to live very long to realize we don't know everything. At times, it seems we know little or nothing about how to connect with the next generations. This verse provides a great visual of God the Father waiting for us to cry out to Him on behalf of our children so He can reveal great and mighty truths that we could never understand on our own. When you pray, be prepared for God to take you to new levels and show you the amazing ways you can influence the next generations.

CHAPTER 9

Blessing the Next Generations

Deuteronomy 30:19 describes the multigenerational influence our actions can have: "I call heaven and earth as witnesses today against you, that I have set before you life and death, blessing and cursing; therefore choose life, that both you and your descendants may live."

The Old Testament provides several examples of one generation blessing the succeeding generations. Perhaps the most memorable biblical blessing is the one David imparts to his son Solomon in **1 Kings 2:1-4**: "Now the days of David drew near that he should die, and he charged Solomon his son, saying: 'I go the way of all the earth; be strong, therefore, and prove yourself a man. And keep the charge of the Lord your God: to walk in His ways, to keep His statutes, His commandments, His judgments, and His testimonies, as it is written in the Law of Moses, that you may prosper in all that you do and wherever you turn; that the Lord may fulfill His word which He spoke concerning me, saying, 'If your sons take heed to their way, to walk before Me in truth with all their heart and with all their soul,' He said, 'you shall not lack a man on the throne of Israel.'"

God has given us the same wonderful privilege to bless our children and grandchildren! However, to bless them in ways that have a lasting effect, we must do so from God's larger vision for our children and grandchildren rather than our limited thinking. Tina Boesch, in her book *Given: The Forgotten Meaning and Practice of Blessing,* speaks to this need: "It occurs to me that the vision required to bless well includes willingness to search my heart and examine my motivations. Am I driven by my own agenda and ambition for my children, or are my blessings shaped by the Lord? Do my words impose my own vision, or free my kids to live in God's grace?"[6] She continues, "The blessing of our children can't be separated from the vitality of our own relationship with God. Blessing begins with seeing both our children and the God who blesses us."[7]

The following paragraphs highlight four powerful and specific ways I believe we can bless the next generation.

We bless the next generation with our words of encouragement. In **1 Kings 2**, David not only spoke a blessing over his son Solomon concerning his desires for Solomon's life, but he also offered specific words of encouragement. In **verses 8-9**, David speaks to Solomon concerning his role in Shimei's life. As part of his instruction, David underscores Solomon's intellectual aptitude, saying, "for you are a wise man." These words greatly encouraged the man who would ultimately become an extraordinarily wise king. Many times, our children and grandchildren need us to speak words that predict a positive future and encourage them to strive for excellence and godly character.

When I sensed a call to vocational ministry at the age of 15, my pastor encouraged me in many ways, one of which was allowing me to speak during a Sunday morning worship service. That sermon was the only one my grandfather (the one who prayed for me beside his bed each night) heard me preach. I saved my sermon notes, and I am grateful everyone did not walk out in the middle of the message! My words were raw and unpolished.

I will always remember my grandfather, a tall and distinguished-looking man, approaching me at the end of the service with a smile on his face. He said, "You did a good job, and I am proud of you." While I knew I had a long way to go as a preacher, I firmly believed God had called me to the ministry. My grandfather's words were a blessing, and they continue to encourage me today. Bless your children and grandchildren with words of encouragement that call them forward and help them believe they can experience all God has in store for them!

We bless the next generation with our conversations. During unscheduled, unscripted discussions, we have the opportunity to pour our experience, wisdom, and values into the next generations. When our girls were young and still living in our home, I often wanted to call a meeting and share my thoughts with them. But my desire to share rarely converged with the girls' desire to listen. More often, a chat about something that occurred at school, a TV show, a family decision, a song on the radio, or a ride to the mall or ballgame would open the door for us to express our thoughts. While my desire to be heard sometimes got in the way of a productive dialogue, I believe the girls caught more truth in those spontaneous moments than they did during intentional meetings and conversations.

One of my daughters recently called me to process something she experienced at church that morning. During the worship service, an announcement was made concerning an important decision the congregation had to make. Though sharing specific information about the decision was appropriate, the announcement focused more on the human capacities, qualifications, and reasons for making the decision than on the congregation's need to seek God's heart and mind about the situation. To my daughter, it appeared the decision had already been made and the vote was simply a formality. As we talked, I asked questions and offered some thoughts. At the end of the conversation, she was ready to move forward. For me, that conversation affirmed this truth: if we ask God to sensitize our hearts to our children's words, He will give us unique opportunities to speak into their lives, even when they are adults. These spontaneous and unscripted moments give us a special opportunity to bless the next generations.

One of the traditions God has used to initiate conversations concerning His activity in our family is the Thanksgiving scrapbook.

FROM DEBBIE

When I was a child, my family gathered at my maternal grandparents' home in North Carolina for Thanksgiving each year. My mom's sister and her family joined us. Since we didn't see each other often throughout the year, the cousins had fun sleeping on pallets on the floor, celebrating Pop's birthday, enjoying a huge Thanksgiving meal, exchanging Christmas presents, putting on plays, giving piano recitals, playing outside in the leaves, and running up the path in the woods to our aunt's house. My grandparents were Christians and valued their family as a gift from God! Unbreakable bonds were being formed. As the cousins grew older, pouring over newspaper ads and Black Friday shopping took the place of playing outside, boyfriends and girlfriends came and went, wives and husbands arrived on the scene, and babies were born. Eventually, we had to gather at Thanksgiving without Mama and Pop.

Several years ago, my cousin Laurie and I felt compelled to document these Thanksgiving gatherings in order to pass down memories of Mama and Pop and their legacy to future generations. We decided to make a scrapbook, adding a new section for each Thanksgiving. With our moms' help, we went as far back as we had pictures and began the scrapbook with the first page focusing on the memory of Mom and Pop. Since we alternate hosting the family gathering each year, the one not hosting makes the scrapbook addition for the previous Thanksgiving. Every year, we take a family picture with four of the youngest children holding big pieces of poster board with the date. We recently began our fourth book! Each year, we pull out all the scrapbooks and spend time laughing, recounting the memories, sharing family stories with the next generations, exclaiming how we've grown, and marveling at all God has done in our family throughout the years. It is a blessing to watch the children enjoy the scrapbooks as much as the adults do.

Laurie and I have told our girls that when we're too old to make the scrapbooks, they must pick up the mantle and keep it going. We have no idea what the scrapbook will look like by then, but we know they wouldn't miss the gathering for anything, and they cherish the legacy that's been passed on to them. We're confident they'll continue the tradition!

We bless the next generation with our example. One of the primary ways we bless the next generations is by setting an example. Simply stated, we must ask God to do first in us what we want to see Him do in our children and grandchildren.

We must remember that our children and grandchildren are watching, listening, and forming opinions, values, and life skills that often imitate what they have seen in us. Betsy describes the powerful impact parents' example can have on their children.

A WORD FROM OUR DAUGHTER

My parents influenced my sister and me in many ways (most of them positive!). While I have numerous childhood memories, my greatest recollection of those years and what I want to carry into my life as a parent of three young children is seeing my parents glorify God by serving people in and through the Church. The principle was evident: love God and love others. I saw my parents model this belief as they mentored other couples or individuals, as Dad wrote his tithe check each week, and as Jamie and I helped Mom deliver food to those who were experiencing challenges.

Perhaps my greatest memory is watching my parents serve others when doing so was inconvenient or uncomfortable. There were plenty of times when it would have been easier just to say "no" or ignore someone's needs, but they were always there to help others no matter the inconvenience. I remember a single mother with two small children who was a member of one of our churches. She was confined to a wheelchair and struggled to complete routine daily tasks. Having the added responsibility of caring for two children must have been harder for her than I can imagine. As Mom talked with Jamie and me one day, it became clear that she felt called to assist this young mother. It was also evident that Mom planned on Jamie and me being part of that help! I remember the woman's house being dirty. It smelled horrible, and a few roaches scurried around as we cleaned. I was probably reluctant to help and unhappy while we were there. But I will never forget those little faces peeking out of the window at us as we drove away and realizing it wasn't about me. It was about helping a family in need, even when doing so was hard.

Today, my husband and I strive to glorify God by ministering to others. I am aware that many in my generation (I am 38) do not see the Church as a channel through which we glorify God and bless others. My generation has been labeled the great "consumer" generation, and we often look to the Church to meet our personal needs, judging a congregation and its leaders by whether we feel served or satisfied. While the Church provides an opportunity for worship, discipleship, and community, it is our responsibility to serve Him and join His activity.

My husband and I try to set a good example at home. We are sinners who mess up daily, yet even on days when we seem to get it all wrong, we must keep pointing our children toward Jesus and "writing on the walls" of our home what God has done for us. Thankfully, in God's grace, there are glimpses of His love shining through our children. We must hold onto those moments and continue the work God has called us to as parents.

Recently, my husband and I, along with my parents, attended the year-end awards day for our daughter's first grade class. When it was time to bestow the Citizenship Award, the teacher described the way the recipient loved and cared for others in practical ways. This student would give her pencil to a child who needed it or share her lunch with someone who had forgotten to bring one. As I listened to the teacher talk about the recipient, I thought, "What a sweet girl she must be!" Then the teacher called our daughter's name and presented the award. What a joy to see the smile on our Leighton's face! I was moved to thank God for honoring what we have been attempting to model for our children at home and for beginning to develop that character trait in their lives.

We bless the next generations with our testimony. One of the most powerful ways we can influence the next generations is by telling them about God's activity in our life. God is always at work around us, and being transparent about our relationship with Him can help our descendants understand that God is more than a doctrine; He is a person who desires to have a love relationship with us. He is practical as well as personal. He works in the mundane moments as well as in larger, more obvious circumstances.

Previously, we addressed the importance of going first. While this principle certainly applies to the example we set with our actions, it also relates to our words. Our children and grandchildren will watch to see if our actions reflect our words. It is impossible to pass along to others something we don't have ourselves.

Psalm 145:4 is extremely relevant to parents and grandparents as we build our spiritual legacy: "One generation shall praise Your works to another and shall declare Your mighty acts." And for this principle to be a reality, we must be intentional. We must purposefully ask God to help us speak in ways that draw our children and grandchildren to Him. I want them to know that God is relevant, and His wisdom, strength, and peace can be part of our lives every day.

At present, I am putting together a written record of God's activity in my life and ministry throughout the past 40 years. It is my account of circumstances, relationships, and decisions God has used to reveal Himself to me. I am focusing especially on Scripture passages God gave me in those moments. I want my family to see how personal

God is and the degree to which He wants to be involved in every aspect of our lives. I plan to share this record with my family (my grandsons are already asking when I am going to have it ready for them to read!) and to continue adding chapters as long as God allows.

CHAPTER 10

Closing Thoughts

I pray these pages have challenged and encouraged you as you seek to join God in a covenant for the next generations. I have experienced great joy, bitter disappointment, perplexing decisions, vacillating emotions, and so much more in my journey as a parent and grandparent. And I believe many pages in my life are yet to be written. While I am an imperfect parent and grandparent, I have found an endless source of help, hope, and wisdom in my loving Heavenly Father, my wife, and the many wonderful mentors and friends God has placed in my path. He adopted me as His child and has been the perfect spiritual parent as He has patiently, clearly, and powerfully revealed what is in His heart and mind for my family. What a privilege it is to partner with the God of the universe to enable each generation to know the Name of the Lord God and live to follow Him.

Perhaps the covenant in your family has been broken. Maybe your family's spiritual legacy will begin with you. If there has been brokenness or lack of legacy, God does not intend for you to feel remorse, anger, or guilt. His desire is for you to find hope and courage as you surrender your life and family to His agenda. Claim the truth of **Jeremiah 29:11** that God has a hope and a future for your family that is far greater than you could ever ask or imagine.

Our awesome, God-assigned role of influencing the next generations hinges on a personal decision in each of our hearts. Are we willing to do whatever it takes to know God's heart and mind? Are we ready to abandon our agenda and surrender to God's plan for our family? Will we live in such a manner that our children and grandchildren want to follow the God they see us serving?

Perhaps you must commit to wake up earlier to spend extra time in prayer and Bible study. Maybe there is an area of your life in which you need to go first and set the example. Are there idols in your life you must renounce? God stands ready to join you in a covenant for the next generations of your family. With God's enabling, it is never too late to build a legacy that honors Him and blesses your children from generation to generation.

END NOTES

1. *Daily Light,* Anne Graham Lotz, Thomas Nelson.

2. *Legacy of Prayer,* Jennifer Kennedy Dean, CrossHouse, pp. 15-17.

3. *Prayer: Finding the Heart's True Home,* Harper Collins, p. 24.

4. *Transforming Prayer,* Daniel Henderson, Bethany House, p. 27.

5. *Transforming Prayer,* Daniel Henderson, Bethany House, p.34.

6. *Given: The Forgotten Meaning and Practice of Blessing,* Tina Boesch, NavPress, p. 50.

7. *Given: The Forgotten Meaning and Practice of Blessing,* Tina Boesch, NavPress, p. 53.

Jennifer Kennedy Dean has been a powerful influence in the lives of many believers, parents and people who pray. Jennifer led prayer conferences at the two churches I pastored in South Carolina and we used her materials many times in small group teaching and in corporate prayer. One of Jennifer's legacies is surely the words of this prayer guide.

– Rick

Praying for Your Descendants

Excerpt taken from *Legacy of Prayer: A Spiritual Trust Fund for the Generations*, by Jennifer Kennedy Dean. © 2010 by The Praying Life Foundation.

1. "If you had responded to my rebuke, I would have poured out my heart to you and made my thoughts known to you" (**Proverbs 1:23**).

Lord, may my descendants respond to Your love, even when it comes in the form of rebuke. Pour out Your heart and cause them to know Your thoughts.

2. "Therefore, I urge you, brothers, in view of God's mercy, to offer your bodies as living sacrifices, holy and pleasing to God—this is your spiritual act of worship. Do not conform any longer to the pattern of this world but be transformed by the

renewing of your mind. Then you will be able to test and approve what God's will is—his good, pleasing and perfect will" (**Romans 12:1–2**).

I pray that my descendants will always stand in full view of Your mercy—that Your mercy will fill their horizon—and that they will joyfully offer themselves as thank offerings, a pleasing aroma to You. May they be transformed from the inside and become living proof that Your will is good, pleasing, and perfect.

3. "The children of your servants will live in your presence; their descendants will be established before you" (**Psalm 102:28**).

May my descendants live in a constant awareness of Your presence, and may they be firmly established before You.

4. "All your sons will be taught by the Lord, and great will be your children's peace" (**Isaiah 54:13**).

*Lord, I pray that You Yourself will be the teacher of my descendants. Lead them into all truth (**John 16:13**), teaching them truth and wisdom in the inner parts (**Psalm 51:6**).*

5. "Send forth your light and your truth, let them guide me; let them bring me to your holy mountain, to the place where you dwell. Then will I go to the altar of God, to God, my joy and my delight. I will

praise you with the harp, O God, my God" (**Psalm 43:3–4**).

Let my descendants be guided by Your Light and Your Truth. May they know Your Son, Jesus, as the Way, the Truth, and the Light. Lead them into such sweet intimacy with You that You are their joy and delight.

6. "Teach me your way, O Lord, and I will walk in your truth; give me an undivided heart, that I may fear your name. I will praise you, O Lord my God, with all my heart; I will glorify your name forever" (**Psalm 86:11–12**).

Give my descendants an undivided heart. May they love you with their whole hearts, with their whole minds, with their whole souls. Draw them so strongly to You that nothing else can lay claim to even a corner of their hearts.

7. "And this is my prayer: that your love may abound more and more in knowledge and depth of insight, so that you may be able to discern what is best and may be pure and blameless until the day of Christ, filled with the fruit of righteousness that comes through Jesus Christ—to the glory and praise of God" (**Philippians 1:9–11**).

Lord, grant to my descendants an abundance of true knowledge and deep insight, and enable them to discern the best in every situation. Let their lives be the branches that display your fruit—the righteousness of Christ.

8. "Not only so, but we also rejoice in our sufferings, because we know that suffering produces perseverance; perseverance, character; and character, hope. And hope does not disappoint us, because God has poured out his love into our hearts by the Holy Spirit, whom he has given us" (**Romans 5:3–5**).

Lord, give my descendants such wisdom in the things of God that they will see their difficulties and hardships as opportunities for You to develop Christlikeness in them. Complete Your full work in their hearts.

9. "For I will pour water on the thirsty land, and streams on the dry ground; I will pour out my Spirit on your offspring, and my blessing on your descendants. They will spring up like grass in a meadow, like poplar trees by flowing streams" (**Isaiah 44:3–5**).

*May my descendants be drenched in Your Spirit. Create in them such a thirst for You that they long for You like a thirsty land longs for water (**Psalm 63:1**).*

10. "Show me your ways, O Lord, teach me your paths; guide me in your truth and teach me, for you are God my Savior, and my hope is in you all day long" (**Psalm 25:4–5**).

Lord, teach my descendants Your paths and Your truth, so that they will place all their hope and expectation in You alone.

11. "Then our sons in their youth will be like well nurtured plants, and our daughters will be like pillars carved to adorn a palace" (**Psalm 144:12**).

Even in their youth, may my descendants have a spiritual strength and maturity that is evident to all.

12. "Direct me in the path of your commands, for there I find delight. Turn my heart toward your statutes and not toward selfish gain" (**Psalm 119:35–36**).

Let my descendants find their delight in Your ways. Keep them from self-centered, self-involved lives, and instead turn their hearts toward You. Give them a passion for You that causes them to honor You in all their ways.

13. "My heart is steadfast, O God" (**Psalm 108:1**).

Give my descendants steadfast hearts, anchored in You, unshakeable and immovable. May my descendants always present a solid phalanx in the army of the Lord.

14. "Keep me from deceitful ways; be gracious to me through your law. I have chosen the way of truth; I have set my heart on your laws" (**Psalm 119:29–30**).

Cause my descendants to set their hearts on Your laws and choose Your way. Let deceitfulness of any kind be foreign to them. May Your grace be the centerpiece of their lives.

15. "They will be called oaks of righteousness, a planting of the Lord for the display of his splendor" (**Isaiah 61:3**).

Let the lives of my descendants be living testimony of who You are.

16. "But they could not stand up against his wisdom or the Spirit by whom he spoke" (**Acts 6:10**).

Lord, may my descendants be so genuinely full of Your Spirit that You will speak through them.

17. "Commit to the Lord whatever you do, and your plans will succeed" (**Proverbs 16:3**).

*Teach my descendants to commit fully their lives to You—taking every thought captive to the obedience of Jesus Christ (**2 Corinthians 10:5**)—so that their plans will reflect Your will, "and the will of the Lord will prosper in his hand" (**Isaiah 53:10**).*

18. "May those who fear you rejoice when they see me, for I have put my hope in your word" (**Psalm 119:74**).

Train my descendants in Your ways, Lord. Teach them early to put their hope in You. Give them experiences that prove that You are true to Your

Word. Let them testify, "Your promises have been thoroughly tested, and your servant loves them" (Psalm 119:140).

19. "Direct my footsteps according to your word; let no sin rule over me. Redeem me from the oppression of men, that I may obey your precepts. Make your face shine upon your servant and teach me your decrees" (**Psalm 119:133–135**).

Set my descendants free from any sinful inclination that may have been passed down through generations. May they live in the freedom that Jesus Christ offers.

20. "I keep asking that the God of our Lord Jesus Christ, the glorious Father, may give you the Spirit of wisdom and revelation, so that you may know him better. I pray also that the eyes of your heart may be enlightened in order that you may know the hope to which he has called you, the riches of his glorious inheritance in the saints, and his incomparably great power for us who believe" (**Ephesians 1:17–19**).

May my descendants have clear spiritual vision to know and understand Your kingdom. Reveal Yourself to them, that they may know You in Your fullness.

21. "Teach me, O Lord, to follow your decrees; then I will keep them to the end. Give me understanding,

and I will keep your law and obey it with all my heart" (**Psalm 119:33**).

May my descendants have both knowledge and understanding in Your Word.

22. "I have heard that the spirit of the gods is in you and that you have insight, intelligence and outstanding wisdom" (**Daniel 5:14–15**).

Lord, I pray that my descendants will be like Daniel. May You be so clearly evident in their lives that unbelievers come to them to discover their secret. Grant them insight, intelligence, and wisdom.

23. "Let salvation spring up, let righteousness grow with it" (**Isaiah 45:8**).

May every one of my descendants come to a saving knowledge of Jesus Christ as his or her Lord and Savior. May their lives be righteous because of You.

24. "May the words of my mouth and the meditation of my heart be pleasing in your sight, O Lord, my Rock and my Redeemer" (**Psalm 19:14**).

*Lord, work mightily in the deep places in the lives of my descendants, creating in them thoughts and ideas and desires that match Yours. Let their hearts be so full of Your living Word that when they speak from the overflow of their hearts (**Luke 6:45**), the words of their mouths will be the words from Your mouth (**John 14:24**).*

25. "I will put my law in their minds and write it on their hearts. I will be their God, and they will be my people" (**Jeremiah 31:33**).

I pray that Your law will be encoded in the spiritual DNA of my descendants. May Your law become their instinctual and spontaneous way of living, more natural to them than unrighteousness.

26. "May your deeds be shown to your servants, your splendor to their children. May the favor of the Lord our God rest upon us; establish the work of our hands for us—yes, establish the work of our hands" (**Psalm 90:16–17**).

Lord, make my life Your theater—a stage upon which You perform. Through my life, may Your splendor be shown to my descendants.

27. "He revered me and stood in awe of my name. True instruction was in his mouth and nothing false was found on his lips. He walked with me in peace and uprightness, and turned many from sin" (**Malachi 2:5–6**).

Let these words, used to describe Levi, be true also of my descendants.

28. "You still the hunger of those you cherish; their sons have plenty, and they store up wealth for their children" (**Psalm 17:14**).

Lord, create in my descendants a hunger and craving for righteousness, a hunger that only You can *satisfy (**Matthew 5:6**). Fill their lives so completely that they discover satisfaction only in You. Fulfill Your promise in their lives that "I will satisfy the priests with abundance, and my people will be filled with my bounty, declares the Lord" (**Jeremiah 31:14**).*

29. "I will give you a new heart and put a new spirit in you; I will remove from you your heart of stone and give you a heart of flesh. And I will put my Spirit in you and move you to follow my decrees and be careful to keep my laws" (**Ezekiel 36:26–28**).

Lord, move my descendants to follow You.

30. "As the deer pants for streams of water, so my soul pants for you, O God. My soul thirsts for God, for the living God. When can I go and meet with God?" (**Psalm 42:1–2**).

Lord, make Yourself irresistible to my descendants, that they will thirst for You.

31. "'Build up, build up, prepare the road! Remove the obstacles out of the way of my people.' For this is what the high and lofty One says—he who lives forever, whose name is holy: 'I live in a high and holy place, but also with him who is contrite and lowly in spirit, to revive the spirit of the lowly and to revive the heart of the contrite'" (**Isaiah 57:14- 15**).

Remove the obstacle of pride from the lives of my descendants. Create in them hearts that are meek and receptive to Your Spirit. Revive them according to Your Word.

ABOUT THE AUTHOR

 *Rick Fisher* serves as Vice President for Blackaby Ministries International. He and his wife Debbie, live in Easley, South Carolina and have two daughters, Jamie and Betsy, sons-in-law Rob and Lucas, and five grandchildren – Thomas, Ashley, Jase, Leighton and Gray.

Rick earned a BA in Religion from Gardner-Webb University and a Master's degree from Southern Baptist Theological Seminary. He has served 30+ years of ministry in the local church (18 years of that as Senior Pastor) and has been part of the BMI team for the past 12 years.

Rick ministers to churches, associations and businesses with focuses in the areas of spiritual leadership, leadership development, Experiencing God, revival/ awakening and prayer/prayer ministry. He is co-author of the book, "*Developing a Powerful Praying Church*".

You can follow him at:

Twitter: **@rickfisher54**
Facebook: **Rick Fisher**

Blackaby Ministries International (www.blackaby.org) is dedicated to helping people experience God. It has books and resources to assist Christians in the areas of experiencing God, spiritual leadership, revival, the marketplace, and the family. There are also resources for young adults and children. Please contact them at:

Facebook:	**Blackaby Ministries International**
Twitter:	**@ExperiencingGod**
Mobile App:	**Blackaby ministries int**
Website:	**www.blackaby.org**

BLACKABY RESOURCES

To discover all the resources BMI offers please see
www.blackabystore.org

BLACKABY LEADERSHIP COACHING

Blackaby Ministries provides coaching-based solutions to challenges faced
by ministry and marketplace leaders. To learn more, go to
www.blackabycoaching.org

BLACKABY REVITALIZATION MINISTRY

If you sense God wants more for your church than what you are currently
experiencing, we want to help.
www.blackaby.org/revitalization

THE COLLISION

God is actively at work in the lives of the younger generation and Blackaby
Ministries is stepping out to join in this exciting activity.
www.thecollision.org

BMI ONLINE CLASSES

Our onlince classes will guide you to a deeper level in your relationship
with God than you have ever experienced before.
www.blackaby.org/onlineclasses

The Collision Vol. 1 demonstrates how Christians can navigate today's increasingly digital and media-driven culture, engage with the crucial conversations happening all around us, and collide head-on with the world for Christ.

Today's Church faces challenges and crises it can only overcome through prayer. Tthe book, Developing a Powerful Praying Church focuses on the adjustments pastors and church leaders must make in their prayer life in order to see a rebirth of God-honoring, world-impacting churches across our nation.

WWW.BLACKABYSTORE.ORG

When God Speaks: How to Recognize God's Voice and Respond in Obedience provides an extensive study of the important truths concerning God's speaking to His people.

DVDs/Videos -- Workbook

These resourcess are produced for the many Christians who have experienced "dry" periods in their life. Many Christian souls have become barren and parched due to life's trials and burdens. The irony is that Christians have living water available within them!

DVDs/Videos -- Workbook -- Trade Book

CPSIA information can be obtained
at www.ICGtesting.com
Printed in the USA
FSHW020322111120